I0086910

Scientists from A to Z

Science Questions and Answers

By Christine Hirsch

How do animals in the woods get ready for winter?

What is the difference between a reptile and an amphibian?

Why did the *T. rex* have sharp teeth?

What do butterflies eat?

How can I sort these bottles?

How can I share what I have discovered?

Why is it cold here but warm in Australia?

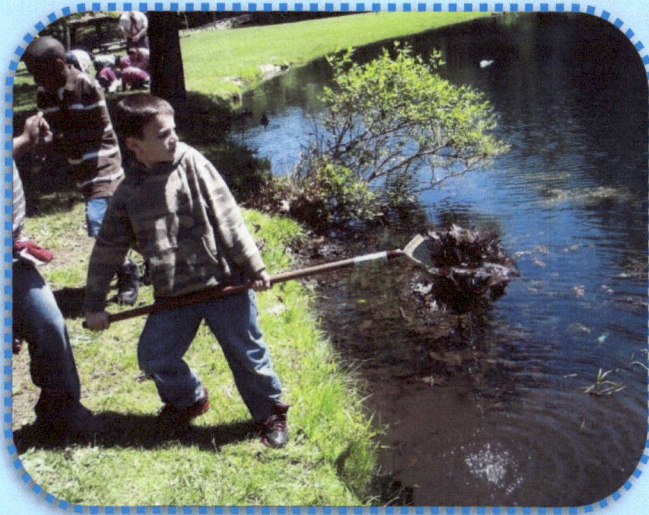

Scientists ask questions and try to find answers.

There are many kinds of scientists who ask different questions.

Which questions can you answer? What kind of scientist are you?

Andy is an **astronomer**. He is using his telescope to look at the moon. "What is the moon made of?" He wonders.

What do you think the moon is made of?

The moon is made of rock and dust. Andy can see the moon's rocky craters and mountains through his telescope.

Brian is a **botanist**. He is measuring a plant. "What can I do to help it grow?" He wonders.

How can Brian help his plant grow?

He can help his plant grow by giving it water and sunlight. The plant makes its own food!

Carla is a **chemist**. She is mixing baking soda and vinegar. "What will happen when they mix?" She wonders.

What do you think will happen?

The mixture will bubble! The bubbles are filled with carbon dioxide gas.

How big is this tree?

Diana is a **dendrologist**. She is looking at a giant sequoia tree. "How big is this tree?" She wonders.

Do you know how big it is?

Giant sequoia trees can grow to be 165 to 280 feet tall and 18 to 24 feet wide!

What do butterflies eat?

Emma is an **entomologist**. She is looking at a butterfly. "What do butterflies eat?" She wonders.

Do you know what butterflies eat?

A butterfly uses its proboscis, a tongue-like body part, to sip juice from flowers or fruit.

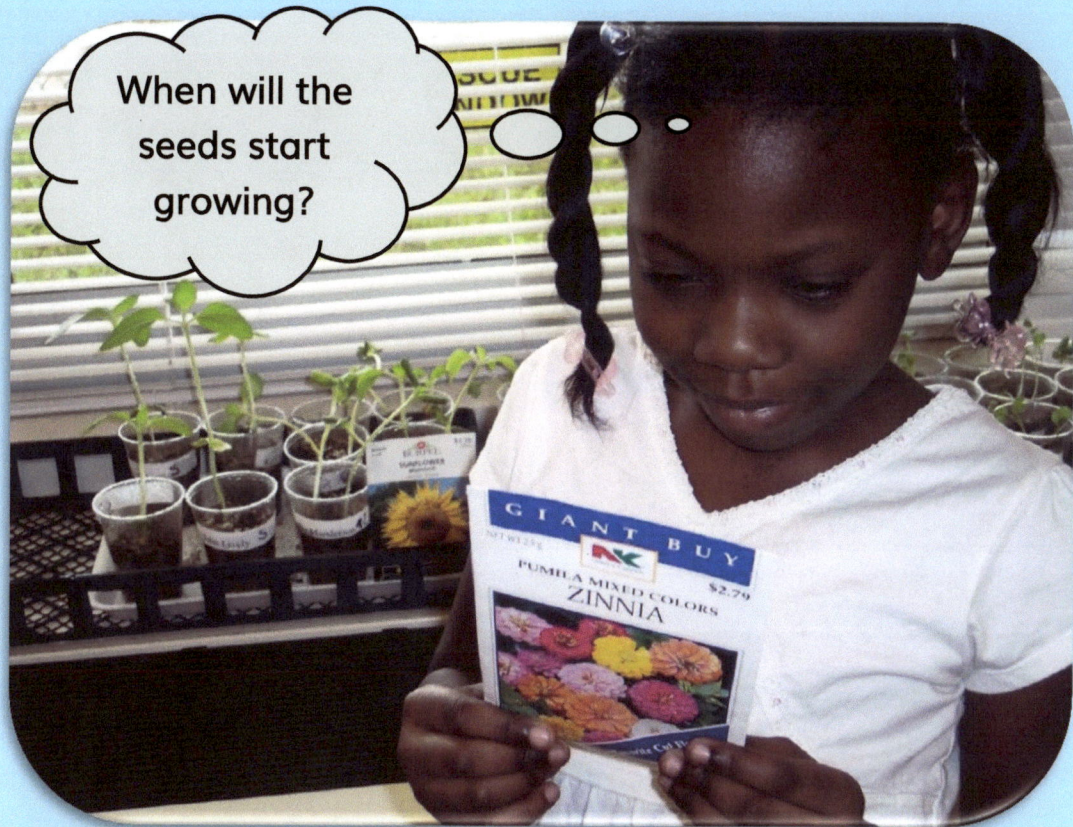

F rancine is a **floriculturist**. She is planting flower seeds. "When will the seeds start growing?" She wonders.

How long do you think it will take before the seeds start to grow?

Francine's flower seeds will germinate, or start to grow, in less than ten days!

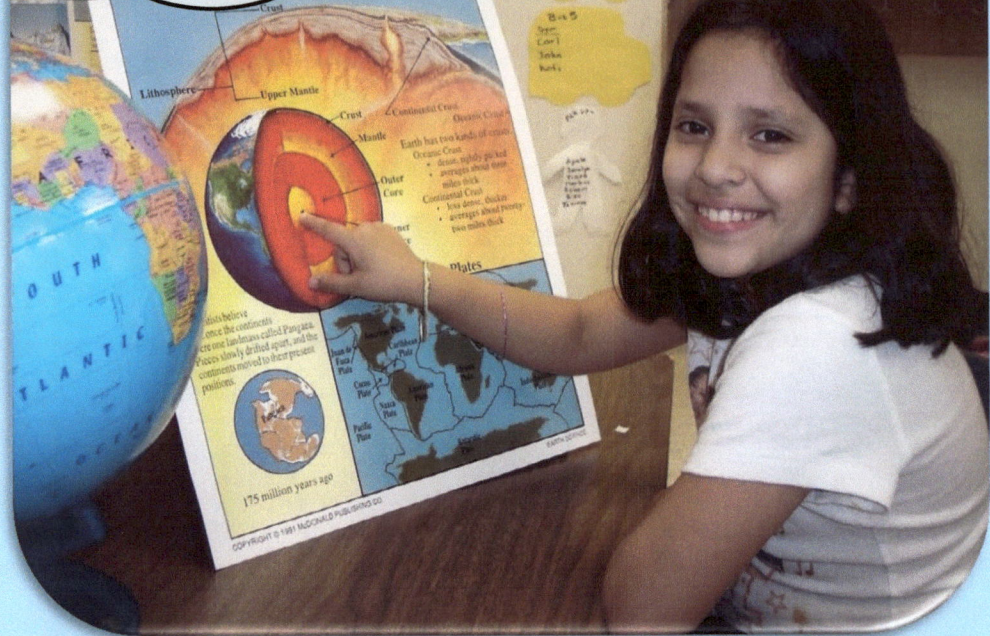

Gina is a **geologist**. She is looking at a model of Earth. "What is at the center of the Earth?" She wonders.

What do you think is at the center of the Earth?

No one has ever been there, but most geologists, or Earth scientists, think the core of the Earth is made of a heavy metal, like iron.

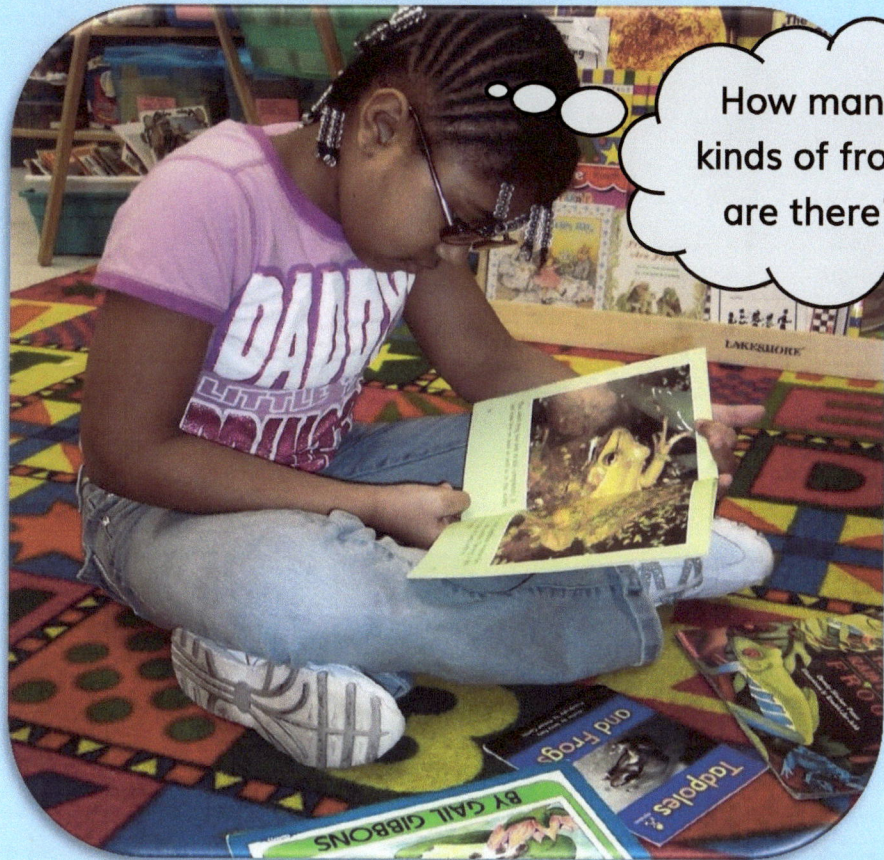

Helen is a **herpetologist**. She is reading about frogs. "How many kinds of frogs are there?" She wonders.

How many different kinds of frogs do you think there are?

There are more than three thousand different kinds, or species, of frogs!

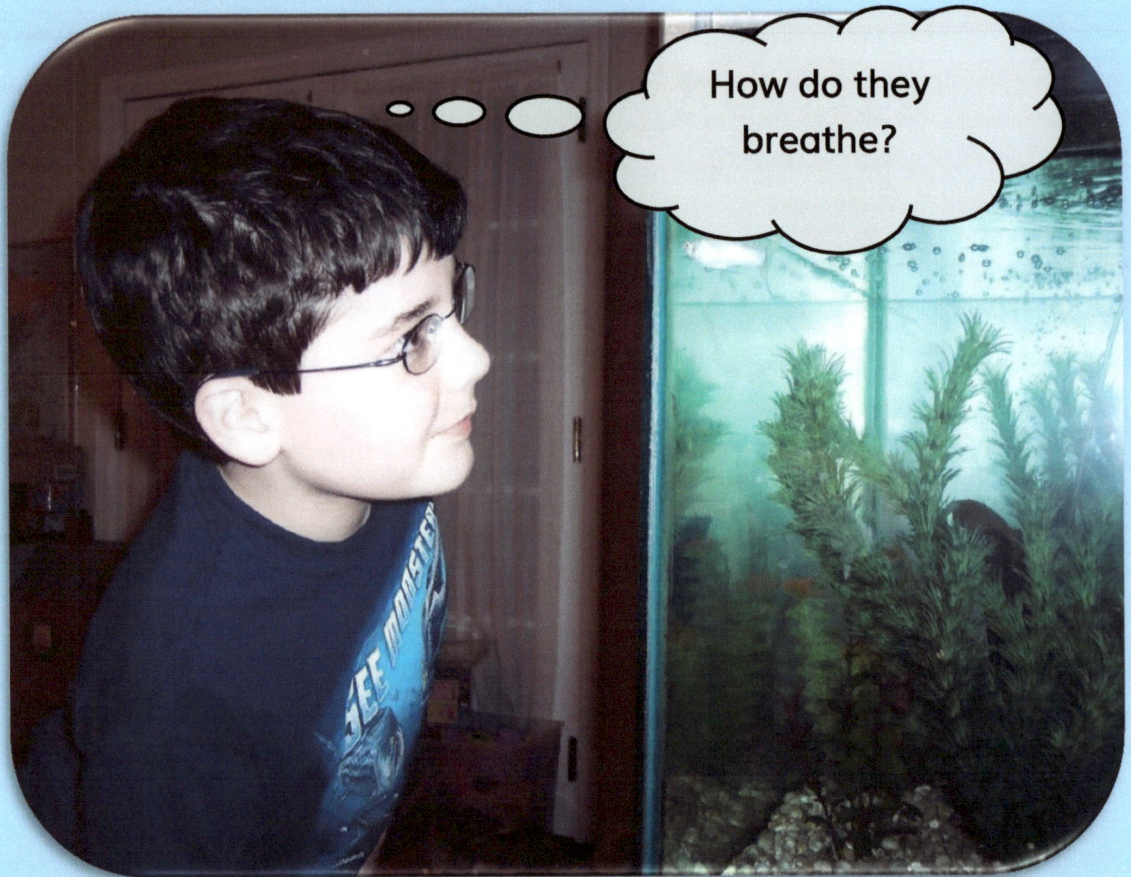

Ian is an **ichthyologist**. He is watching fish swim in the aquarium. "How do they breathe?" He wonders.

Do you know how fish breathe?

Fish use their gills to breathe. The gills take oxygen out of the water. They are like our lungs, which take oxygen from the air.

Jason is a **journalist**. He is writing about his scientific discoveries. "How can I share what I have discovered?" He wonders.

How do you think he can share information with other people?

Scientists share reports they have written with other scientists in scientific journals, on the internet or at science fairs. Scientists often use charts and graphs to show what they've discovered.

> What causes a hockey puck to move so quickly across the ice?

Kelli is a **kineticist**. She is watching a hockey puck move. "What causes it to move so quickly across the ice?" She wonders.

Why do you think the puck moves so easily?

The ice is smooth, so the puck slides easily. There is very little friction, or roughness, on the smooth ice.

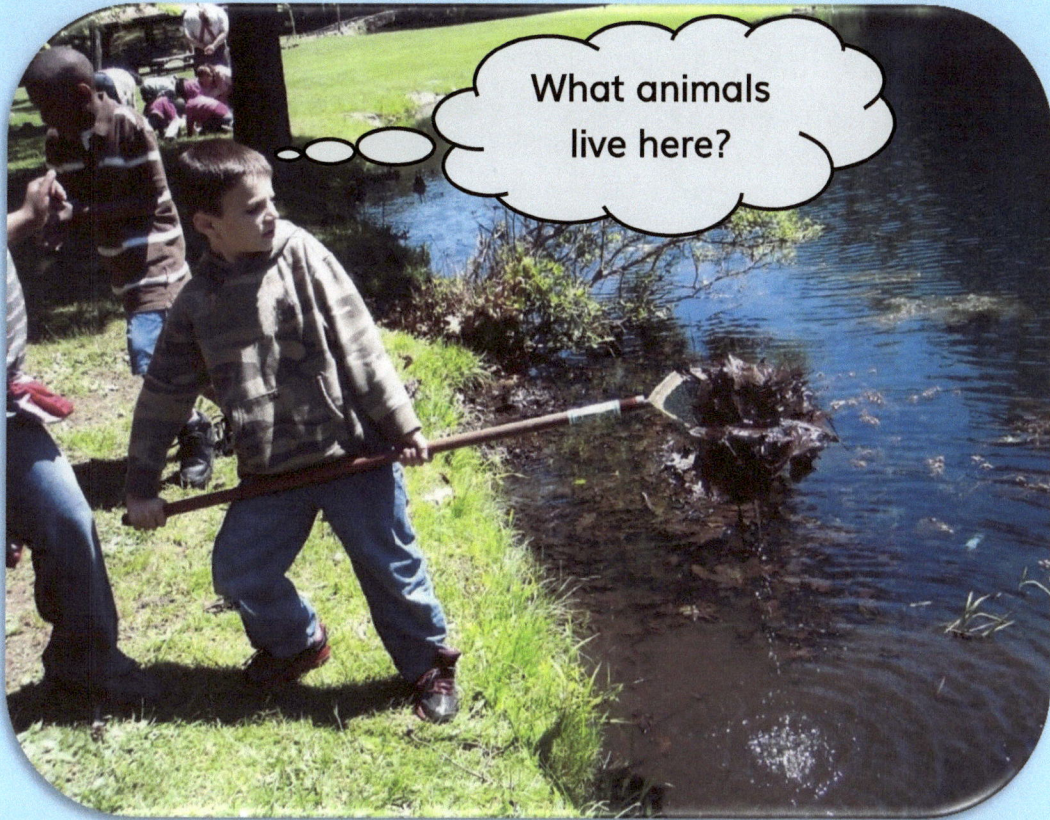

Lloyd is a **limnologist**. He is looking at mud and leaves from the lake bottom.

"What animals live here?" He wonders.

What animals do you think he will find?

Lloyd finds snails, dragonfly nymphs, tiny clams, frog eggs, tadpoles and bottom-feeding fish. He lives in the northeastern United States. Depending on where you live, you may find different animals.

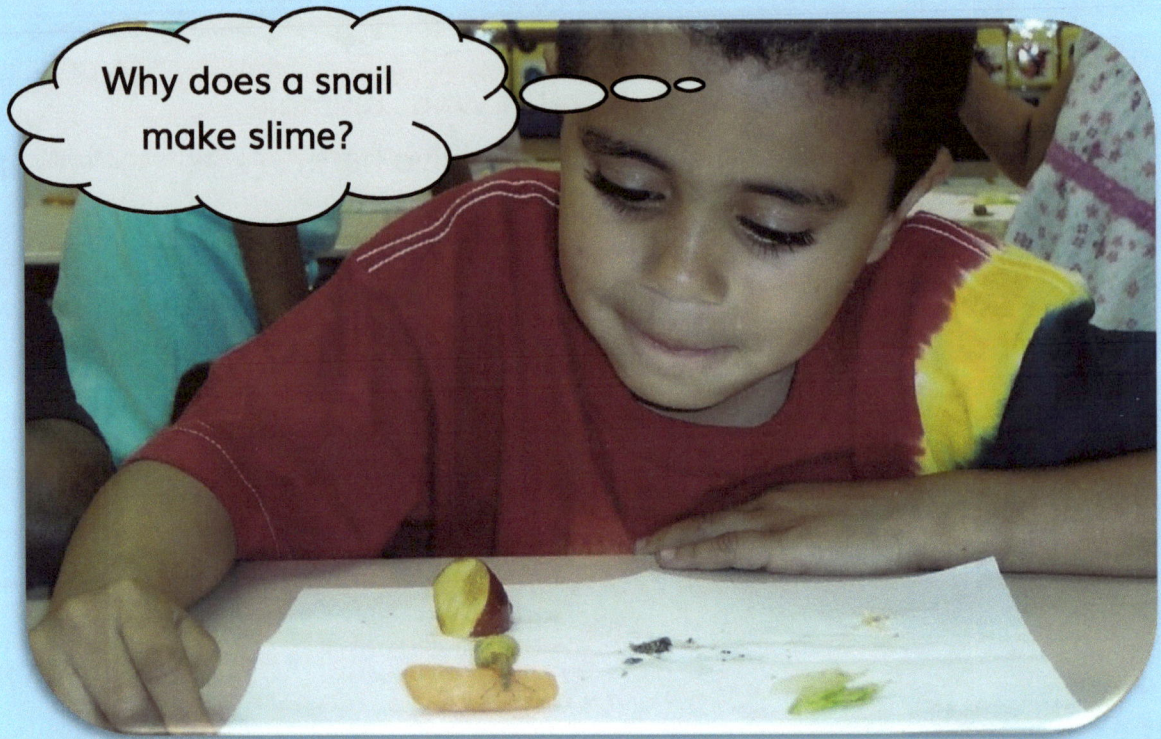

Why does a snail make slime?

Malcolm is a **malacologist**. He is looking at the slime trail a snail makes as it moves.
"Why do snails make slime?" He wonders.

Do you know why snails make slime?

Snails make slime when they move. The slime trail helps snails slide easily because it makes the surface smooth. The amount of slime needed depends on the roughness of the surface — a snail makes more slime when moving on sandpaper than glass.

How do animals in the woods get ready for winter?

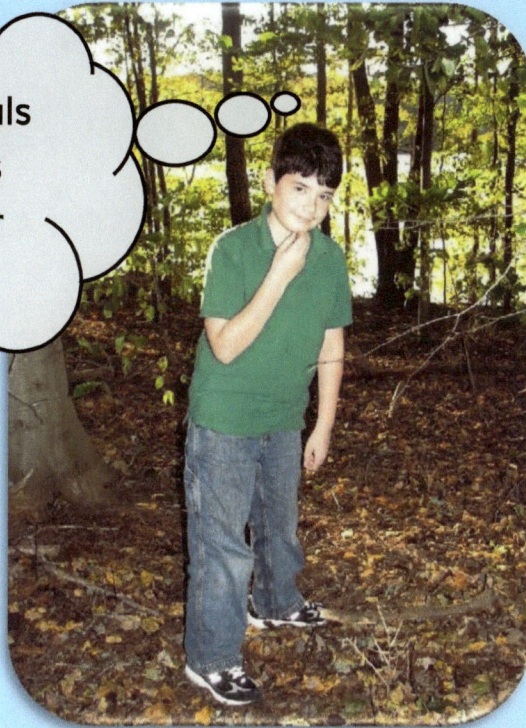

Nathan is a **naturalist**. He is walking in the woods.

"How do animals in the woods get ready for winter?" He wonders.

Do you know how animals get ready for winter?

To survive long, cold winters, some animals migrate, or move to warmer places. Others hibernate, or sleep for long periods of time. Still others stay active all winter. These animals often store food and grow more fur to keep warm.

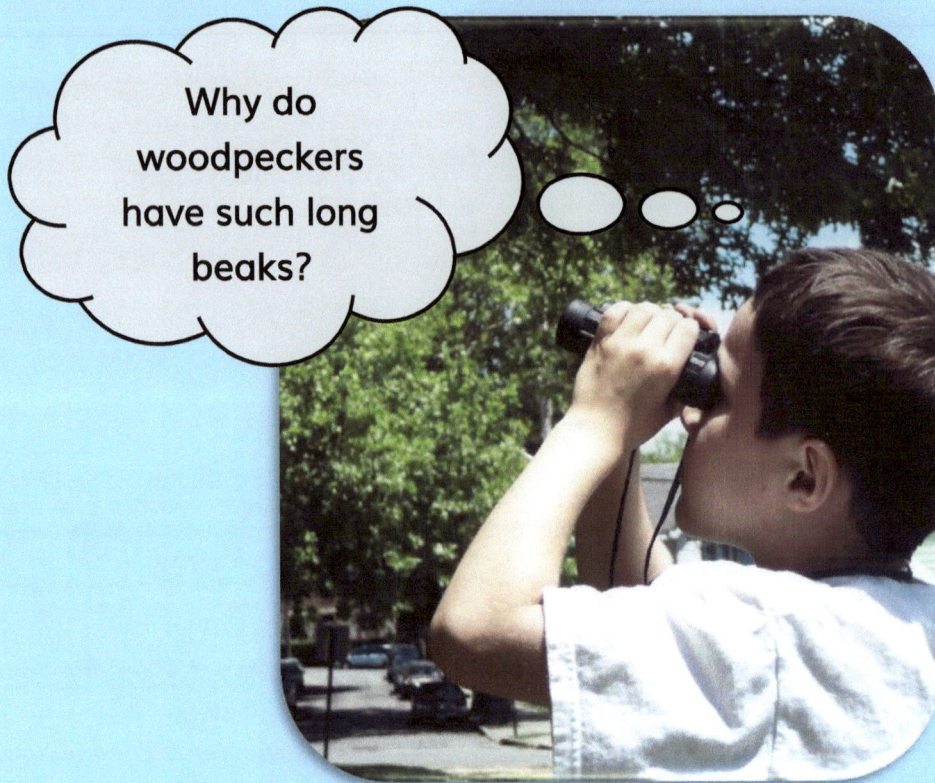

Oscar is an **ornithologist**. He is watching birds.

"Why do woodpeckers have such long beaks?" He wonders.

Do you know why woodpeckers have long beaks?

A woodpecker uses its long, pointed beak to dig out a nest and to get food, such as insects that live under tree bark. Some woodpeckers, also called sapsuckers, drill small holes with their beaks to get the sap to flow so they can drink it.

Why did the *T. rex* have sharp teeth?

Paula is a **paleontologist**. She is looking at fossils of dinosaur bones. "Why did the *T. rex* have sharp teeth?" She wonders.

Why do you think the *Tyrannosaurus rex* had sharp teeth?

The *Tyrannosaurus rex* was a carnivore and needed sharp teeth to eat meat. The *T. rex* had more than sixty teeth. Some *T. rex* teeth were nine inches long!

Quinten asks **questions**. All scientists ask questions. "Why is the sky blue?" He wonders.

Do you know why the sky looks blue?

The light from the sun is made up of a rainbow of colors, but the air around the Earth, our atmosphere, does not let all the light pass through. It traps the blue light, making the sky look blue.

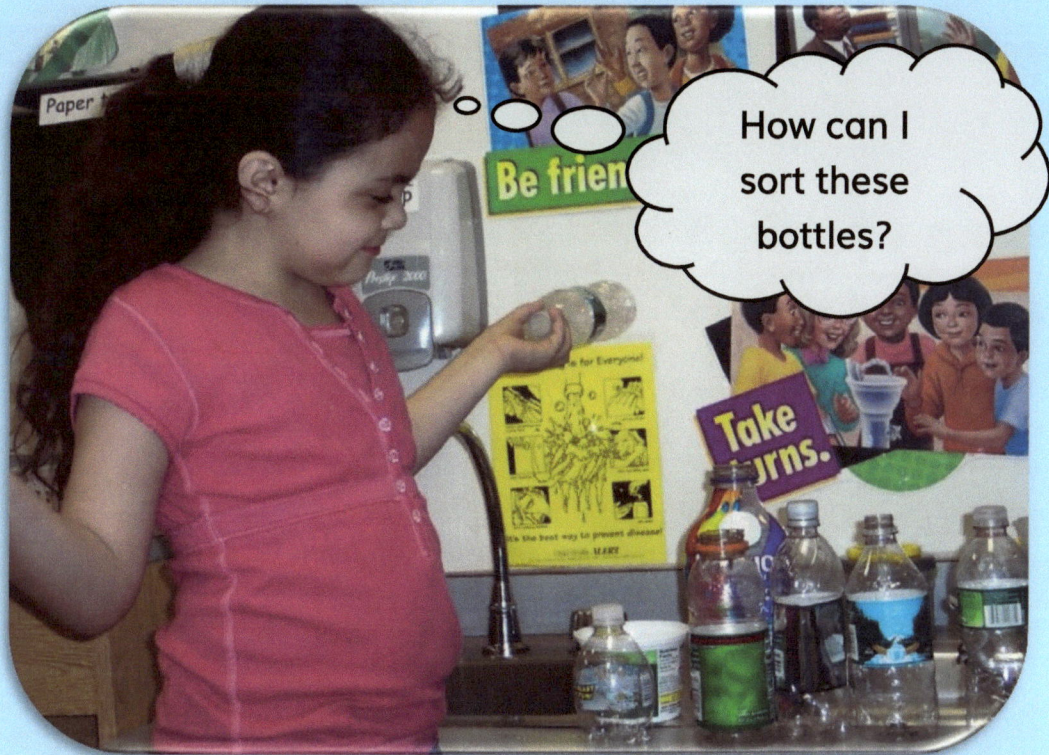

Regina is a **recyclist**. She is reusing plastic bottles. "How can I sort these bottles?" She wonders.

Do you know how plastic is sorted at recycling centers?

Plastic is sorted by whether it sinks or floats. Type 1 plastic will sink in water. Type 2 plastic will float. Try it! Cut some plastic bottles into half-inch squares, put them in water and see which ones float.

Stacy is a **speleologist**. She is exploring a cave.

"How big is the largest cave in the world?" She wonders.

How big do you think it is?

The largest cave in the world, Mammoth Cave in Kentucky, is more than four hundred miles long!

What will happen when I heat chocolate?

Tina is a **thermochemist**. She is cooking.

"What will happen when I heat chocolate?" She wonders.

What do you think will happen to the chocolate?

The solid chocolate will change to a liquid state. When it cools, it will change back into a solid.

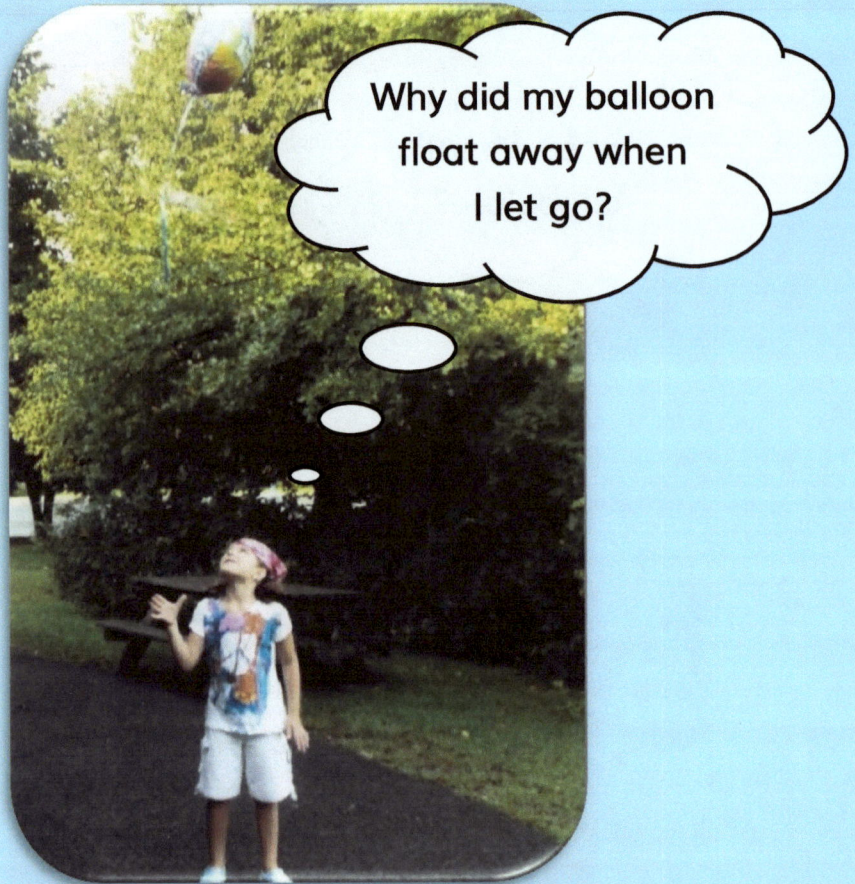

Why did my balloon float away when I let go?

Ursula is trying to **understand** something.

Scientists try to understand things. "Why did my balloon float away when I let go?" She wonders.

Why did Ursula's balloon float away?

The balloon is filled with helium gas. It is lighter than the gases in the air. That is why it floats.

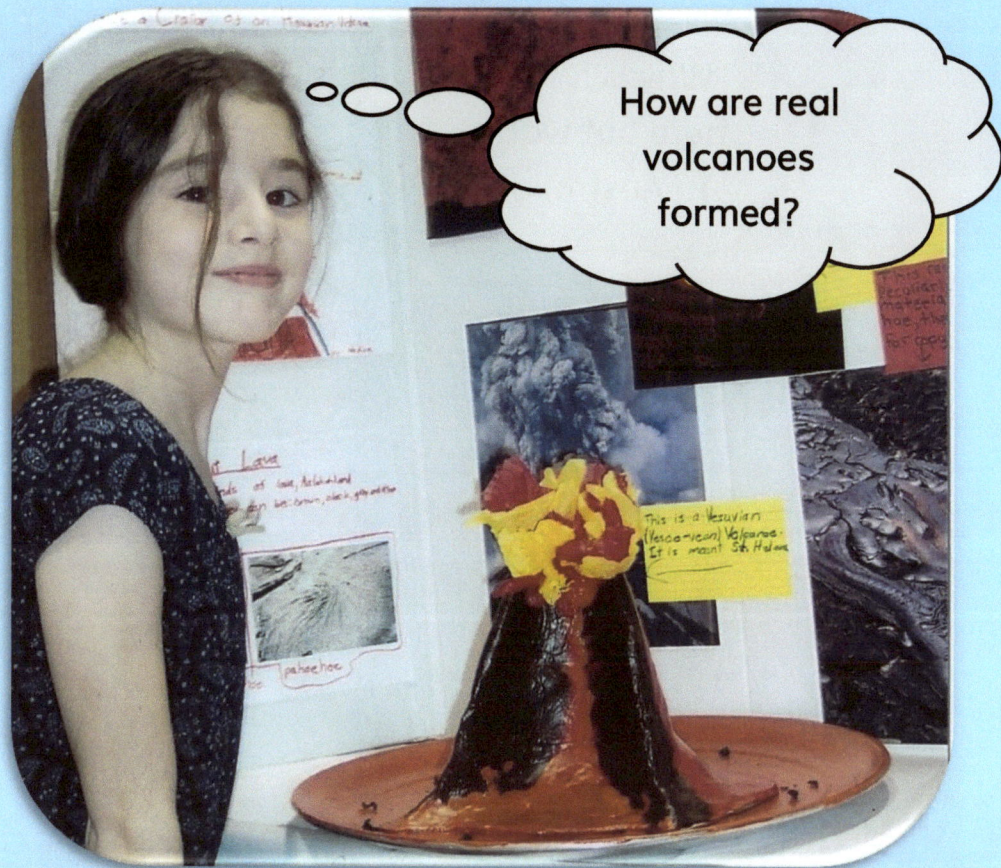

Victoria is a **volcanologist**. She is looking at a model of a volcano. "How are real volcanoes formed?" She wonders.

Do you know how volcanoes are formed?

Gas and melted rock, called magma, come through weak spots in the Earth's crust. Over time, the hardened lava builds up to make a cone-shaped mountain.

Why is it cold here but warm in Australia?

Wanda is **wondering**. All scientists wonder.

"During January, why is it cold in New York where I live but warm in Australia where my pen pal lives?" She wonders.

Do you know why?

When the Northern Hemisphere, where New York is, is tilted away from the sun, the Southern Hemisphere, where Australia is, is tilted toward the sun. Tilting closer to the sun gives the people in Australia warm weather, while the people in New York are having cold weather.

Which foil boat will hold more pennies?

Xavier is **experimenting**. Scientists conduct experiments to test their ideas.
"Which foil boat will hold more pennies: the flat one or the one with sides?" He wonders.

Which do think will hold more pennies?

Try it! Take a four-inch square of aluminum foil and shape it into a boat. Keep another piece of foil flat. Float them both in water. Put pennies on your boats one at a time and see which one holds more. You can try different types of designs to see what works best.

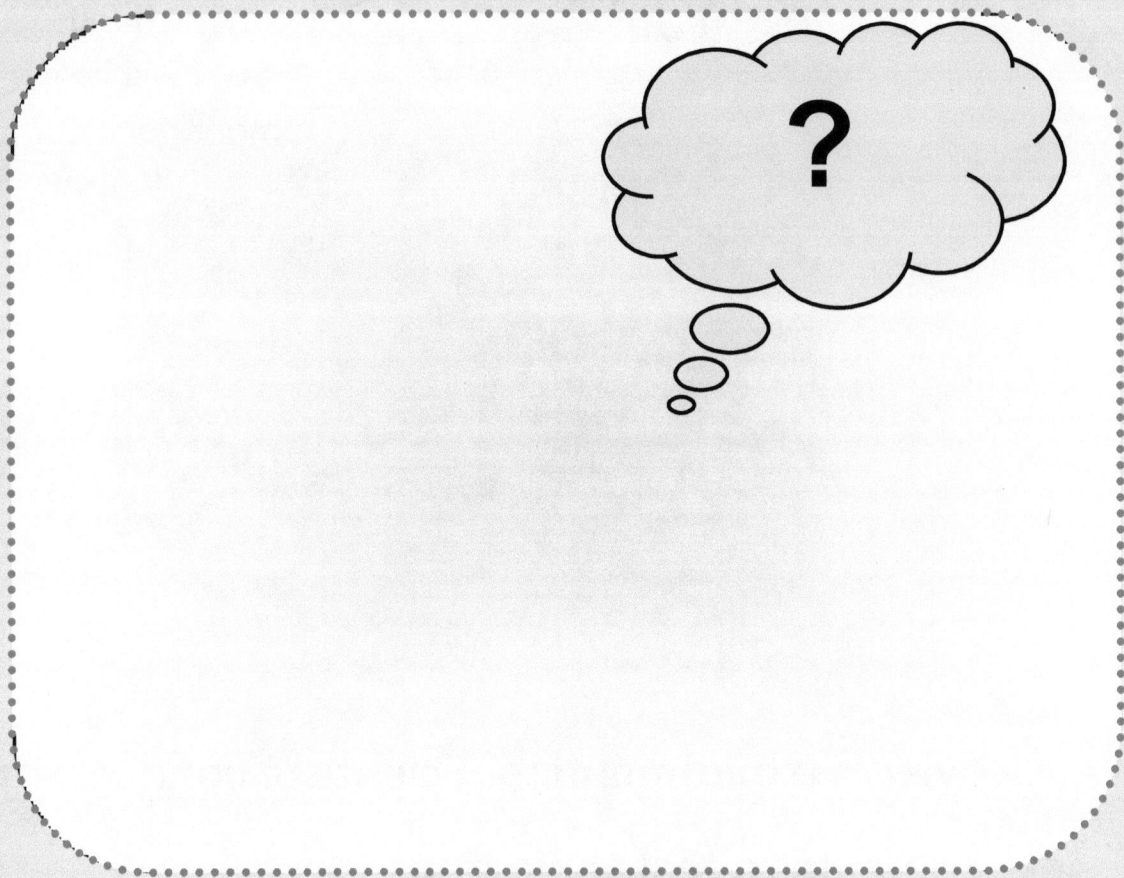

You are a scientist!

What do you wonder about?
What questions do you ask?

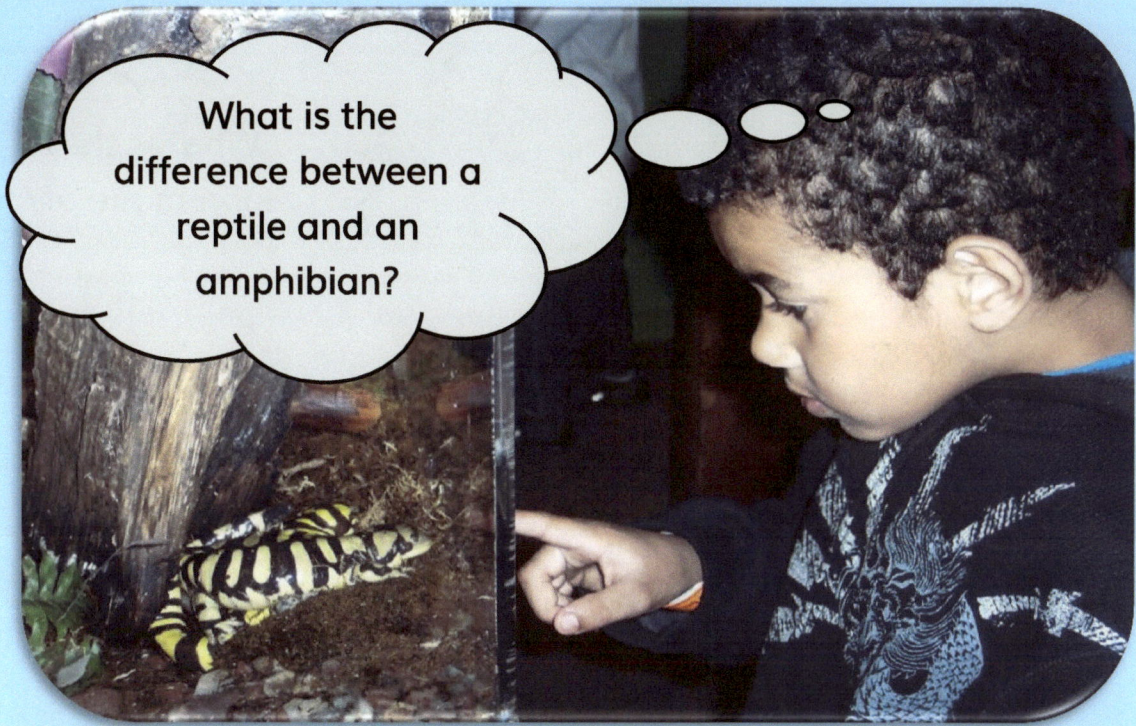

Zack is a **zoologist**. He is observing an animal.

"What is the difference between a reptile and an amphibian?" He wonders.

Do you know the difference?

There are many differences, but one difference is amphibians start out life with gills and then develop lungs for breathing later. Reptiles have lungs for breathing from birth.

What is at the center of the Earth?

What is the moon made of?

When will the seeds start growing?

Why did my balloon float away when I let go?

What will happen when I heat chocolate?

Why is the sky blue?

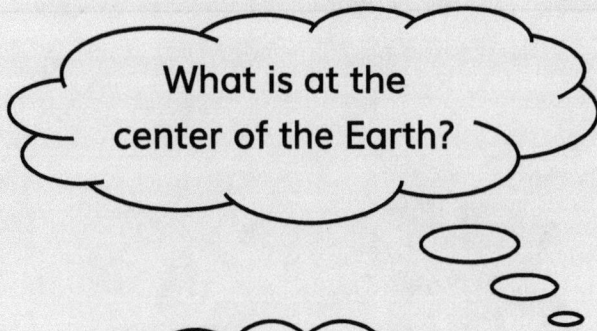

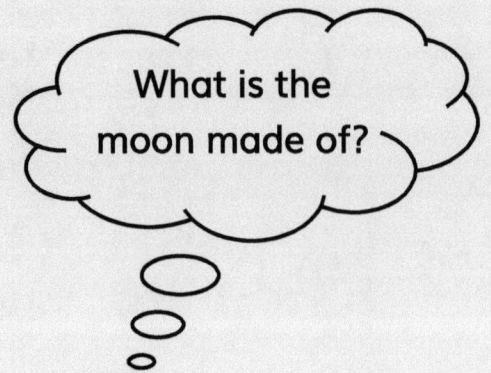

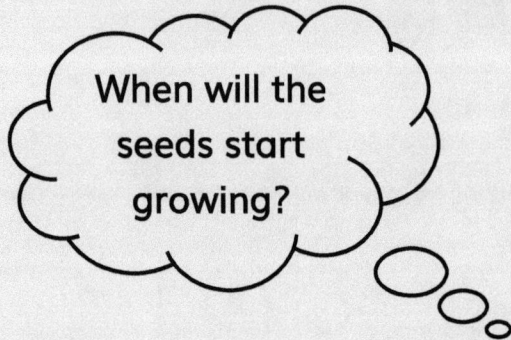

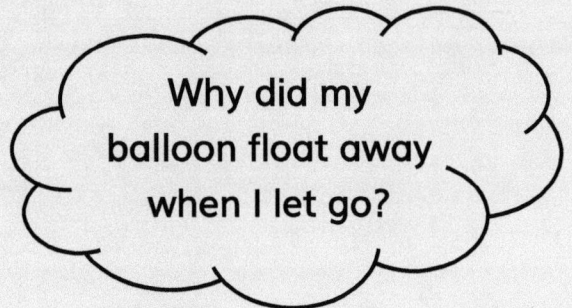

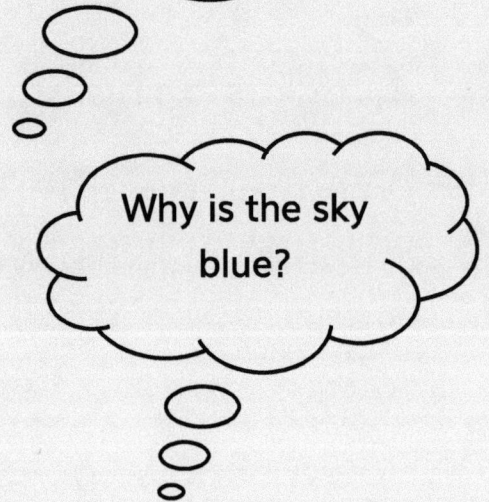

What do you like to learn about?
What do you wonder about?

What kind of scientist are you?

Scientists from A to Z

Astronomer (uh-stron-*uh*-mer) a scientist who studies space

Botanist (bot-n-ist) a scientist who studies plants

Chemist (kem-ist) a scientist who studies forms of matter

Dendrologist (den-drol-*uh*-jist) a botanist who studies trees

Entomologist (en-t*uh*-mol-*uh*-jist) a scientist who studies insects

Floriculturist (flawr-i-kuhl-cher-ist) a scientist who studies flowering plants

Geologist (jee-ol-*uh*-jist) a scientist who studies the origin of the Earth along with its rocks, minerals, and landforms

Herpetologist (hur-pi-tol-*uh*-jist) a zoologist who studies reptiles and amphibians

Ichthyologist (ik-thee-ol-uh-jist) a zoologist who studies fish

Journalist (jur-nl-list) a person who keeps a record of events

Kineticist (ki-net-*uh*-sist) a scientist who studies movement

Limnologist (lim-nol-uh-jist) a scientist who studies bodies of fresh water, such as lakes or ponds

Malacologist (mal-uh-kol-uh-jist) a zoologist who studies mollusks such as snails, shellfish, slugs, octopuses, and squids

Naturalist (nach-*er*-uh-list) a person who studies plants and animals in their natural environment

Ornithologist (awr-n*uh*-thol-*uh*-jist) a zoologist who studies birds

Paleontologist (pey-lee-*uh*n-tol-*uh*-jist) a scientist who studies life from the past through the study of animal and plant fossils

Recyclist (ree-sahyk-list) a person who reuses things

Speleologist (spee-lee-ol-*uh*-jist) a scientist who studies caves

Thermochemist (thur-moh-*kem*-uhst) a chemist who studies heat related to chemical reactions and changes of state

Volcanologist (vol-k*uh*-nol-*uh*-jist) a scientist who studies volcanoes

Zoologist (zoh-ol-*uh*-jist) a scientist who studies animals

www.ingramcontent.com/pod-product-compliance
Lightning Source LLC
Chambersburg PA
CBHW041239040426
42445CB00004B/90